MARIO

and the Hole in the Sky
HOW A CHEMIST SAVED OUR PLANET

Elizabeth Rusch
Illustrated by Teresa Martínez

ini Charlesbridge

For all who choose science over silence—E. R.

To all future scientists—T. M.

Text copyright © 2019 by Elizabeth Rusch
Illustrations copyright © 2019 by Teresa Martínez

At the time of publication, all URLs printed in this book were accurate and active.
Charlesbridge, the author, and the illustrator are not responsible for the content or accessibility of any website.

Published by Charlesbridge
85 Main Street
Watertown, MA 02472
(617) 926-0329
www.charlesbridge.com

Library of Congress Cataloging-in-Publication Data
Names: Rusch, Elizabeth, author. | Martínez, Teresa, 1980– illustrator.
Title: Mario and the hole in the sky: how a chemist saved our planet / Elizabeth Rusch; illustrated by Teresa Martínez.
Description: Watertown, MA : Charlesbridge, [2019]
Identifiers: LCCN 2015026828 | ISBN 9781580895811 (reinforced for library use) | ISBN 9781632898579 (ebook)
| ISBN 9781632898586 (ebook pdf)
Subjects: LCSH: Molina, Mario J.—Juvenile literature. | Chemists—Biography—Juvenile literature. | Nobel Prize winners—
Biography—Juvenile literature. | Ozone layer depletion—Juvenile literature. | Atmospheric ozone—Juvenile literature. |
Air—Pollution—Juvenile literature.
Classification: LCC QD22.M665 R87 2019 | DDC 363.738/75 [B]—dc23
LC record available at https://lccn.loc.gov/2015026828

Printed in China
(hc)   10 9 8 7 6 5 4 3 2 1

The artwork was created digitally using Photoshop and a Wacom tablet.
Display type set in Neue Neueland TF by Treacyfaces
Text type set in Adobe Garamond Pro by Adobe Systems Incorporated
Color separations by Colourscan Print Co Pte Ltd, Singapore
Printed by 1010 Printing International Limited in Huizhou, Guangdong, China
Production supervision by Brian G. Walker
Designed by Martha MacLeod Sikkema and Susan Mallory Sherman

*M*ario Molina was born in Mexico City on March 19, 1943. By the time he was six, the world was awash in amazing new products made from amazing new chemicals.

Spray. Spray. *Mario's mother misted perfume onto her wrist.* Squirt. Squirt. *Someone polished a window.* Spurt. Spurt. *A press of a button propelled cleaner onto a counter, paint onto a fence, and hair spray onto curls.*

But one of the new chemicals, used in millions of spray cans and refrigerators, had a dangerous side that no one had yet discovered. . . .

"¡*Feliz cumpleaños*, Mario!" On Mario's eighth birthday his parents gave him a microscope.

Mario peered through the lens at a drop of water.

Boring, he thought. Then he began to wonder: *What would happen if I looked at dirty water?*

Mario soaked some lettuce and let it rot. After a few days the gooey, brownish-green mess smelled awful. Mario plugged his nose, sucked up a dropper of the filthy water, and dripped it onto a slide. He peered into the lens and gasped.

"*¡Increíble!* All these amazing creatures in just one drop of water!"
Mario studied everything he could under the microscope: sparkling
salt crystals, tomatoes, onions, chilies from salsa—even toothpaste.
Mario was itching to see more.

"Can I use this bathroom as a laboratory?" he asked his parents. "No one ever uses it."

"*¡Dios mío!*" his mother groaned. "Sounds messy."

But they removed the toilet for him and installed some shelves.

"Don't blow anything up," his father warned.

Clink, clink. Hissss. Whoosh! Bitter-smelling smoke wafted out from under the door of Mario's bathroom lab.

"What are you up to, Mario?" asked his aunt Esther, who was a chemist.

"Look at this, *Tía.*" He showed her what scorched detergent looked like on a slide.

She smiled and said, "I think you need a few more things." She brought him a Bunsen burner and chemicals not found in a kids' chemistry set.

Mario carefully mixed potions in his bathroom lab. Miraculously, substances changed from black to yellow, from water soluble to waterproof.

He conducted more experiments with a chemistry teacher in boarding school in Switzerland. He burned chemicals over the flames of Bunsen burners. Sparks flashed purple-pink, crimson-red, and green-blue like fireworks.

To Mario chemistry had a mysterious power—a power that was changing the world around him. Stores were full of NEW AND IMPROVED PRODUCTS featuring REMARKABLE NEW INGREDIENTS that promised to be CHEAPER, BETTER, and EASIER!

But Mario knew that even chemicals that seemed harmless could react with things in the environment and become dangerous. As Mario continued his study of chemistry, a question nagged at him: Were these new chemicals really safe?

Soon after getting his PhD and beginning work in the United States, Mario heard something that started him on a quest to find out.

A scientist studying air samples found tiny amounts of chlorofluorocarbons, or CFCs, floating around in the air. Mario knew CFCs were used in refrigerators, air conditioners, insulation, and fast-food containers, and as a propellant in millions of spray cans. He and his colleague F. Sherwood Rowland wondered: Once CFCs were sprayed into the air or leaked out at the dump, what happened to them?

Mario and Sherry set up a bunch of experiments to find out.

They mixed CFCs with water. Most chemical compounds dissolve in rain. But the CFCs didn't dissolve.

They shone lights on CFCs. Some chemical compounds break down when light shines on them. But the CFCs didn't break down.

They set up a contraption to mimic Earth's lower atmosphere, where any surviving chemical compounds usually decompose. But still the CFCs endured.

SUN

In the upper atmosphere a layer of ozone surrounds our planet. Like a powerful sunscreen, the ozone layer filters out deadly solar radiation, known as ultraviolet light. "What would happen if CFCs reached the ozone layer?" Mario asked.

To answer the question, Mario grabbed the simplest tools of a chemist: a pencil and paper. He jotted down the ingredients that could be released if radiation broke down CFCs:

- carbon, called C
- fluorine, called F
- chlorine, called Cl

Solar radiation hits CFC.

Chlorine breaks off.

ATMOSPHERE

Freed chlorine crashes into ozone.

Ozone breaks up.

Then he wrote down what would happen if those ingredients reacted with the oxygen, called O, in ozone (O_3).

Mario discovered something scary.

Chlorine floating around, freed by radiation, would break up ozone.

Bent over his chemical equations, Mario felt a huge weight pressing on him. The problem was even worse. After the chlorine destroyed ozone, the chlorine survived. It could float around and destroy more and more ozone. Just one atom of chlorine could knock out tens of thousands of molecules of ozone!

Without ozone, deadly solar radiation would bombard Earth, killing all plant and animal life.

Mario hurried to Sherry's office. "We have a problem, a serious problem, and we have to do something."

Mario and Sherry faced a sea of TV and newspaper reporters. CFCs used in millions of products are destroying our ozone layer, they said. They tried to explain the chemistry behind it. But only a few news reports followed—and none captured the magnitude of the crisis.

Mario tried again. He told Congress that CFCs were destroying the ozone layer. Still no one took action. No one seemed to understand how serious the problem was.

Mario was aghast. "People believed it was just impossible that humankind could endanger the entire planet. The planet was big enough. It would just take care of itself," he says. "But I knew this wasn't true."

"A LOAD OF RUBBISH.

"IT'S A SCIENCE-FICTION TALE."

For more than ten years, Mario continued to study the problem and warn people about the danger. "If we keep using CFCs," he said, "huge chunks of the ozone layer will thin or disappear. Skin cancer and eye disease could surge. Crops could fail. It could be a catastrophe!"

Chemical companies, newspapers, even other scientists said horrible things about Mario. Someone even accused him of being a spy trying to cause chaos in America.

"But why in the world would I make this up?" Mario thought. "I'm a SCIENTIST."

He never gave up.

"UTTER NONSENSE."

Then a British scientist took some measurements of ozone in the atmosphere. He found something strange. There seemed to be a huge hole in the ozone over the Antarctic—a hole the size of the United States.

People wondered how that could happen. How could we have so much impact on our atmosphere—and so quickly? Mario and Sherry again tried to explain the chemistry.

Still, people demanded more proof. Scientists launched an expedition
to Antarctica, counting chlorine and ozone from a high-flying airplane.
The results were clear—and horrifying.
Chlorine was definitely destroying ozone.
Finally, people believed the scientists. Something had to be done.
But what?

Leaders from countries all over the world flocked to Montreal, Canada, to discuss the problem. Mario explained the science. He pleaded for nations to join together to stop the destruction of the ozone layer. "The discussions were so slow and cumbersome," he says. "I worried that they might not succeed."

Representatives returned to their countries across the globe. Mario returned to his home in the United States and waited. "This was the Earth's first global issue," says Mario. "There really was no example of the whole planet taking action on something like this before. I didn't know what would happen."

Then Mario heard the news. Twenty-eight countries, including the United States and Mexico, agreed to stop making CFCs. Soon, forty-six countries agreed. Then more than 190 countries—nearly every country in the world—agreed to the Montreal Protocol. "It was thrilling and satisfying and very much a relief," Mario says.

For a while CFCs already floating around in the air continued to rise to the ozone layer. But Earth slowly makes ozone all the time. Once the barrage of CFCs lessened, the ozone layer began to recover. It is expected to heal completely by 2070.

Humans had created the first global environmental problem—and they found a way to fix it.

Now when Mario visits his hometown of Mexico City, where pollution clouds his view of a snow-capped volcano, he worries about another invisible problem: global warming. The burning of oil, coal, and gas is changing the world's climate at a terrifying pace.

But Mario has hope for our planet. His work on the ozone layer has shown that nations, together, can solve global problems. "We can work with all countries, all cultures, all peoples of the world," he says. "We *can* work together. It *is* possible.

"We saved our planet once. We can do it again."

EPILOGUE: Mario Takes on Global Warming

Mario Molina in 2013.
Photo credit: Erik Jepsen, UC San Diego.

On October 11, 1995, Mario Molina was in his office preparing to teach a chemistry class. *Brrring*. The call was from Sweden. Mario, Sherry Rowland, and atmospheric scientist Paul J. Crutzen had won the Nobel Prize in Chemistry for their work on CFCs and the ozone layer. "I was just stunned. I was just so surprised, I couldn't believe it," Mario recalls. Mario's students celebrated by serenading him with a mariachi band.

"I slowly realized that winning the Nobel Prize and all the attention one gets—I could put that to good use," he says. And he has.

Mario donated two hundred thousand dollars of his Nobel Prize money to the Massachusetts Institute of Technology for a fellowship program for young scientists from developing countries. "You never know which young, bright mind holds the solution to a serious problem we face in the world," he says. "We need every one."

Then he turned his attention to another big environmental problem: global warming. Scientists had discovered that the burning of fossil fuels such as coal, oil, and natural gas was releasing "greenhouse gases" into the atmosphere. These gases trap heat, warming the planet and causing global climate change. The more Mario learned, the clearer it became: the world is warming at a dangerous rate, and human actions are to blame.

True, replacing fossil fuels is more difficult than replacing CFCs. "But we do have solutions," Mario says. "What we need is for most of the countries to agree, just like they did with the ozone layer, that the problem is so serious that we have to solve it using everything in our power."

Mario has gathered with other scientists to urge the world to act quickly to prevent further global warming. They have advised the US Supreme Court to support regulation of carbon-dioxide emissions from cars. And Mario has counseled presidents of the United States and Mexico on environmental policy, encouraging them to participate in the first international effort to slow global warming.

In 2016 the world began to address the problem. As part of the Paris Agreement, 195 nations promised to reduce carbon emissions. The goal is to keep global temperature change under 2°C. Mexico promised a 25 percent drop in carbon emissions by 2030. The United States pledged to reduce greenhouse emissions 26 to 28 percent by 2025—and President Barack Obama followed up with efforts to support clean power and curtail tailpipe emissions. Mario and fellow scientists called the agreement "a small but historic and vital first step towards more enlightened stewardship of Earth's climate system."

But President Donald Trump, who has repeatedly called climate change a hoax, intends to withdraw from the Paris Agreement as soon as the agreement allows. Withdrawal would become official in November 2020.

Mario and twenty-nine other scientists advised the Trump administration against withdrawal. "Most of the climate warming over at least the last six decades has been . . . due to the burning of fossil fuels and other human activities," they wrote. "If we continue to increase the atmospheric levels of greenhouse gases, the Earth will continue to heat up, with serious consequences for economies and ecosystems across the globe."

But they rang a note of hope. "Just as science has diagnosed the cause of the changes in the Earth's climate system, science can also provide the basis for solutions," they said.

Many citizens in the United States are not waiting for the federal government to take needed steps. Thousands of state governors, city mayors, and business CEOs have promised to keep working to meet the Paris Agreement carbon-emissions targets.

We fixed the ozone crisis. We can end global warming, too. But we need to commit to solving the problem together.

> **"Climate change is perhaps the most worrisome global environmental problem confronting human society today."**
>
> —Mario Molina, speaking before the US Senate Committee on Energy and Natural Resources

SURPRISING SIMILARITIES:
The Ozone Hole and Global Warming

Global warming is not the first instance of humans endangering the planet. The threat to the ozone layer was eerily similar. We may be in the thick of the global-warming problem now, but our experience with the ozone hole suggests that a solution is within our reach.

THE OZONE HOLE

THE PROBLEM

CFCs damage the ozone layer.

THE THREAT TO OUR PLANET

Damage to the ozone layer lets in dangerous solar radiation, which endangers all plant and animal life.

THE SCIENCE

Solar radiation in the upper atmosphere hits a CFC molecule and breaks off one chlorine atom. The chlorine atom (Cl) reacts with ozone (O_3), breaking off one oxygen atom and destroying the ozone molecule. Equation: $Cl + O_3 \rightarrow ClO + O_2$

When the ClO molecule, called chlorine monoxide, collides with an oxygen atom (O), the chlorine atom breaks free. Equation: $ClO + O \rightarrow Cl + O_2$

The chlorine atom is now ready to destroy another ozone molecule. One chlorine atom can destroy 100,000 molecules of ozone.

THE DELAY

Ozone depletion was called an unproven hypothesis, a hoax, and a fraud. Little was done about the problem for a decade.

GLOBAL EFFORTS

The United States, the biggest producer of CFCs, led the international effort to ban CFCs. More than 190 countries have signed on to the Montreal Protocol.

SCIENTIFIC CONSENSUS

By 1986 most scientists agreed that CFCs destroy ozone and that something should be done.

THE HOPE

Natural processes will remove excess chlorine from the atmosphere, and natural ozone production will restore the ozone layer to normal. Ozone above Antarctica is already recovering.

THE OUTCOME

CFC emissions have been halted.

SOLUTIONS

Stop making and using CFCs.

GLOBAL WARMING

THE PROBLEM
Burning of coal, oil, and natural gas releases gases that trap heat, warming the planet.

THE SCIENCE
Sunlight passes through the atmosphere and warms Earth's surface. Normally, Earth radiates some of the heat back out into space. But burning fossil fuels releases carbon dioxide (CO_2) and other greenhouse gases, which act like a blanket around the planet, holding in heat. As the greenhouse gases collect in the atmosphere, the planet gets hotter and hotter.

THE THREAT TO OUR PLANET
Rising temperatures have begun to melt glaciers, raise sea levels, cause mass extinctions of plants and animals, and increase severe weather such as heat waves, flooding, and drought.

THE DELAY
Global warming has been called an unproven hypothesis, a hoax, and a fraud. Little has been done about the problem for decades.

GLOBAL EFFORTS
Almost 200 countries, including the United States, signed the Paris Agreement, promising to work to keep global temperatures from rising more than 2°C. But President Donald Trump intends to withdraw the United States from the agreement as soon as the treaty allows.

SCIENTIFIC CONSENSUS
Almost all climate scientists agree that the burning of fossil fuels is warming the planet and that something should be done.

THE OUTCOME
Greenhouse gases continue to pour into the atmosphere.

SOLUTIONS
Reduce the burning of fossil fuels and capture greenhouse gases. Conserve energy. Develop energy sources that don't release carbon dioxide, such as solar, wind, and even wave power.

THE HOPE
All nations, including the United States, will act quickly to permanently reduce the amount of greenhouse gases released into the atmosphere. If they do, the global climate will eventually stabilize and return to normal.

READ MORE
About Mario Molina and the Ozone Layer

Guidici, Cynthia. *Mario Molina.* Chicago, IL: Raintree, 2006.

Kent, Deborah. *Mario Molina: Chemist and Nobel Prize Winner.* Chanhassen, MN: Child's World, 2004.

Martins, John. *Ultraviolet Danger: Holes in the Ozone Layer.* New York: Rosen Publishing Group, 2006.

Morgan, Sally. *The Ozone Hole.* New York: Franklin Watts, 1999.

Nardo, Dan. *Ozone.* Farmington Hills, MI: KidHaven, 2006.

The Ozone Hole: http://www.theozonehole.com
  Includes links to news on the ozone hole, graphics and videos, and a history of the ozone problem and the
  Montreal Protocol.

Understanding Science/Ozone Depletion: http://undsci.berkeley.edu/article/0_0_0/ozone_depletion_01
  Details how discovery of the ozone problem reflects the scientific process.

About Global Warming

Basher, Simon. *Basher Science: Climate Change.* New York: Kingfisher, 2015.

Cherry, Lynne, and Gary Braasch. *How We Know What We Know About Our Changing Climate: Scientists
  and Kids Explore Global Warming.* Nevada City, CA: Dawn Publications, 2008.

Cole, Joanna. *The Magic School Bus and the Climate Challenge.* New York: Scholastic, 2010.

Collard, Sneed B., III. *Hopping Ahead of Climate Change: Snowshoe Hares, Science, and Survival.* Missoula,
  MT: Bucking Horse, 2016.

David, Laurie, and Cambria Gordon. *The Down-to-Earth Guide to Global Warming.* New York:
  Orchard, 2007.

Heos, Bridget. *It's Getting Hot in Here: The Past, Present, and Future of Climate Change.* Boston: HMH
  Books for Young Readers, 2016.

Climate Kids (NASA): https://climatekids.nasa.gov
  Kid-friendly facts, videos, and games—even descriptions of green careers.

Climate Reality Project: https://www.climaterealityproject.org
  Watch videos on climate change, sign up for a training, or invite a climate-change leader to present
  at your school.

Global Climate Change (NASA): https://climate.nasa.gov
  Vital signs keep you up to date on the effects of global climate change.

Paris Agreement: https://unfccc.int/process/the-paris-agreement/what-is-the-paris-agreement
  Learn essential elements of the agreement and monitor its progress.

Skeptical Science: https://www.skepticalscience.com
  Understandable presentation of scientific information to help you talk with the many Americans who
  doubt that global warming is a problem.

The URLs listed here were accurate at publication, but websites often change. If a URL doesn't work, you
can use the internet to find more information.

DO MORE!

There are things you can do today—and every day—to use less energy and release less greenhouse gas into the atmosphere.

- Instead of driving in a car, walk, ride your bike, or use public transportation whenever possible.
- Turn off lights and all other appliances and gadgets when you're not using them.
- Ask your parents to replace incandescent light bulbs with LEDs or compact fluorescent bulbs.
- Reuse and recycle materials whenever you can. (Making new things requires energy.)
- Plant a tree. (Trees consume carbon dioxide and release oxygen.)
- Learn more about global warming and share what you know with your family and friends so they take steps to solve the problem, too.

AUTHOR'S NOTE: The Research Process

I was an elementary-school student when I first heard that common, everyday products could damage a layer around our planet that protects us from deadly solar radiation. To me, the ozone problem felt a little unbelievable and very scary. I was relieved when I learned that the whole world banned CFCs and that our ozone layer would recover.

When I first heard about global warming, the problem felt familiar. Global warming also seems hard to believe and scary. That's why I wanted to write a book about the ozone hole—to remind readers that we have faced a similar challenge before and we *can* fix this.

As I began researching the ozone hole, I learned about Mexican American chemist Mario Molina, his childhood interest in chemistry, his role in discovering and solving the ozone problem, and his ongoing work on global warming. I decided that his story would be a perfect way to tell the story of the ozone problem and what it means for global warming.

The best part about writing a nonfiction biography of a living subject is that the person can tell you his or her story, describe important things that happened, and answer questions.

Before interviewing Dr. Molina by phone, I read dozens of newspaper and magazine articles and books about him and about CFCs and the ozone problem. I read the articles in chronological order to get a sense of how the story unfolded in the news. In the mid-1970s, articles such as "Why Aerosols Are Under Attack" (*Business Week*, February 17, 1975) captured the first indications that scientists had discovered a serious problem. The 1980s were all about questioning whether CFCs were really dangerous, as you can see in articles such as "CFCs and Ozone: Deadlocked" (*The Economist*, November 28, 1981). After the huge ozone hole over the Antarctic was discovered, the news articles shifted to agreement on the problem and action to address it ("Worldwide Pact Sought on Ozone" by Philip Shabecoff, *The New York Times*, February 19, 1987). Articles in the 1990s celebrated Mario Molina's Nobel Prize ("MIT Scientist Shares Nobel for Identifying Ozone Damage" by David L. Chandler, *The Boston Globe*, October 12, 1995). And more recent articles tell of Dr. Molina's ongoing work for the environment ("Socially Responsible Science" by Olive Heffernan, *Nature*, October 11, 2012, and "Turning Up the Heat" by Patricia Smith, *New York Times Upfront*, April 21, 2014).

To understand the science and the politics of ozone depletion and global warming, I also read websites such as the United Nations site on ozone (http://ozone.unep.org) and NASA's site on global climate change (https://climate.nasa.gov).

I even read really difficult, technical scientific-journal articles such as "Stratospheric Sink for Chlorofluoromethanes: Chlorine Atom-Catalysed Destruction of Ozone" by Mario J. Molina and F. S. Rowland (*Nature*, June 28, 1974). (I had to read some of this material multiple times to understand it.)

I wanted to know what Dr. Molina told government officials, so I reviewed Congressional testimony, such as *Statement of Mario Molina, Professor, University of California, to the U.S. Senate Committee on Energy and Natural Resources, July 21, 2005*.

All that background reading gave me details about Dr. Molina's life and work and helped me outline the story. But I wanted to know much more about Dr. Molina's childhood, how his interest in chemistry developed, how the ozone problem unfolded, and how he felt each step of the way. So I drafted a long list of questions and interviewed Dr. Molina by phone in May and July of 2008 and again in January 2014.

All quotations not on the list below come from my interviews with Dr. Molina. Most are direct quotations. The others come from parts of the interviews where I asked Dr. Molina to try to reconstruct what people said or thought in some important times in his life, especially his childhood.

With Dr. Molina's approval I translated a few phrases into Spanish to better capture the culture of those scenes. Most likely the dialogue in all the scenes from his childhood was in Spanish.

Source Notes

Pages 24–25: "[It's] a science-fiction tale," "A load of rubbish," and "Utter nonsense": Ozone-crisis skeptics quoted by Patrick McCurdy in "Fluorocarbons: Still Time for a Fair Shake, Not Bum's Rush" (*Chemical Week*, July 16, 1975).

Page 35: "a small but historic . . . climate system": Mario Molina and other scientists in "An Open Letter Regarding Climate Change from Concerned Members of the U.S. National Academy of Sciences," September 20, 2016.

Page 35: "Most of . . . the globe" and "Just as science . . . solutions": Mario Molina and other scientists in their open letter to Scott Pruitt, administrator of the US Environmental Protection Agency, March 13, 2017.

Page 35: "Climate change . . . today": Mario Molina in his testimony before the US Senate Committee on Energy and Natural Resources, July 21, 2005.

Author's Appreciation

My enormous thanks go to Dr. Mario Molina for taking time from his important work to share his story with me and young readers. My gratefulness also extends to the many people who helped make this a better, more accurate, more engaging book: research assistants Elizabeth Bartholomew, Michelle Blair, Melissa Dalton, Erin Dees, Elizabeth Goss, and Erika Schnatz; writers Addie Boswell, Judy Cox, Ruth Feldman, Ellen Howard, Barbara Kerley, Amber Keyser, Michelle McCann (and her students at Portland State University), Lori Mortensen, Sabina Rascol, Lori Ries, Nicole Schreiber, and Emily Whitman; and most of all to kid readers Sydney Dunn, Madison Fassiotto, Gabrial Lafond, Jacob Mesch, Cobi Rusch, Illiana Schuring, Zackary Schwartz, and Stacy Rosoff's third-grade class at the Chapman Elementary School in Portland, Oregon. Thanks, too, to editors Alyssa Mito Pusey and Yolanda Scott and the whole Charlesbridge team for their unfailing support through a difficult time and for their deep commitment to bringing this story to young readers. It is an honor to work with you all. My warmest thanks to the brilliant Teresa Martínez for her vibrant illustrations, which breathe life and humanity into this complex—but important—story.

TIME LINE

1928
Thomas Midgley Jr. and Charles Franklin Kettering invent a colorless, odorless, nonflammable, noncorrosive "miracle compound" called chlorofluorocarbon (CFC), or Freon.

1967
Mario earns a postgraduate degree from the University of Freiburg in Germany.

1968–1972
Mario earns his doctorate in chemistry from the University of California, Berkeley.

1974
Mario and Sherry publish their findings on CFCs and ozone in the journal *Nature*.

1975
Mario becomes a citizen of the United States.

1930 **1940** **1950** **1960** **1970**

1930s
Commercial production and use of CFCs begins.

1943
José Mario Molina-Pasquel Henríquez is born in Mexico City on March 19.

1960–1965
Mario studies chemical engineering at the University of Mexico.

1973
Mario begins teaching and conducting research at the University of California, Irvine, with F. Sherwood "Sherry" Rowland.

1974
Mario and Sherry hold a press conference at the American Chemical Society in Atlantic City, New Jersey.